# I Wonder Why

# The Dodo Is Dead

## and other questions about extinct and endangered animals

### Andrew Charman

KINGFISHER
a Houghton Mifflin Company imprint
222 Berkeley Street
Boston, Massachusetts 02116
www.houghtonmifflinbooks.com

First published in hardcover in 1996
First published in this format in 2007
10 9 8 7 6 5 4 3 2 1
1TR/0607/SHEN/RNB(RNB)/126.6MA/F"
Copyright © Larousse plc 1996

LIBRARY OF CONGRESS CATALOGING-IN-PUBLICATION DATA
Charman, Andrew.
I wonder why the dodo is dead and other questions about extinct
and endangered animals. 1st American ed.
p. cm.—(I wonder why)
Includes index
Summary: Answers questions about extinct animals
and animals in danger of becoming extinct, with a focus
on reasons for endangerment and conservation efforts.
1. Endangered species—Juvenile literature.
2. Extinct animals—Juvenile literature.
[1. Endangered species.
2. Extinct animals. 3. Questions and answers.]
I Title. II. Series: I wonder why (New York, N. Y.)
QL83.C48 1996
591.52'—dc20  96-182 CIP AC

ISBN 978-0-7534-6095-5

Printed in Taiwan

Series editor: Clare Oliver
Series designer: David West Children's Books
Cover Illustration: David Wright (Kathy Jakeman)
Cartoons: Tony Kenyon (B. L. Kearley)
Consultants: Andrew Branson, Michael Chinery

# CONTENTS

# Why are there no dinosaurs on Earth?

● Animals can become extinct because of things that people do, or because the places they live in change.

The dinosaurs lived on Earth for millions of years. Then 65 million years ago, they became extinct—every single one of them disappeared. No one knows exactly why, but one idea is that the world became too cold for them. Whatever the reason, there are no dinosaurs alive today.

# Do all animals die out?

Every kind, or species, of animal dies out eventually. New animals usually appear to replace these animals. The new ones are often descendants of the extinct ones. For example, elephants on Earth today are related to the hairy mammoths, which died out long ago.

● Many animals are endangered—that is, in danger of dying out—because people have hunted too many of them, or are still hunting them.

● When harmful chemicals get into the air, soil, or water, they can cause pollution. This can poison so many animals that the species become endangered.

● When people move to new parts of the world, they often take animals with them. These new animals sometimes hunt the ones that already live there.

● Some kinds of animals are endangered because the places in which they live are cleared to make room for farms, factories, roads, or houses.

# Why is the dodo dead?

Dodos lived on the island of Mauritius in the Indian Ocean until they all died out in about 1680. Many were killed by hungry sailors who visited the island. The poor birds weren't used to hunters and were too slow to escape.

- The elephant bird was the largest bird that's ever lived. Its eggs were 200 times bigger than a chicken's egg. It died out about 300 years ago.

- The dodo laid its eggs on the ground, which made them easy pickings for hungry dogs or rats!

# Which extinct animal looked half-horse, half-zebra?

Herds of fast-running quaggas once roamed the grassy plains of southern Africa. But they were shot by settlers for their unusual skins and for meat. So many were killed that by 1883 there was not a single quagga left.

● In England, 160 years ago, it was fashionable to have a team of quaggas pulling your carriage.

● The last Tasmanian tiger, or thylacine, was seen 60 years ago. It was a strange mixture: it looked as if it had the head of a wolf, the stripes of a tiger, and the tail of a kangaroo!

# How many insects are there?

So far, we have found around one million different kinds of insects—that's more than any other type of creature. Yet many insects are at risk of extinction. If we go on destroying their homes, many insects will die out—some before they've even been discovered.

● The rare Queen Alexandra's birdwing butterfly lives in Papua New Guinea. But its forest home is being cleared for farming.

● There are so many insects it is impossible to look after each one. The best way to save them is to protect the places where they live.

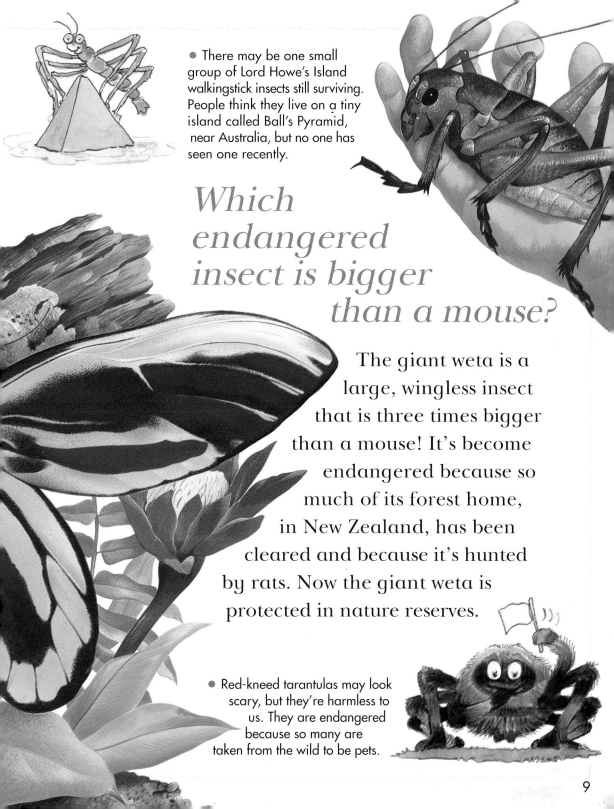

• There may be one small group of Lord Howe's Island walkingstick insects still surviving. People think they live on a tiny island called Ball's Pyramid, near Australia, but no one has seen one recently.

# Which endangered insect is bigger than a mouse?

The giant weta is a large, wingless insect that is three times bigger than a mouse! It's become endangered because so much of its forest home, in New Zealand, has been cleared and because it's hunted by rats. Now the giant weta is protected in nature reserves.

• Red-kneed tarantulas may look scary, but they're harmless to us. They are endangered because so many are taken from the wild to be pets.

# Why do animals like wetlands?

Animals such as dragonflies, turtles, beavers, and storks live in wetlands—wet, boggy places, such as streams, marshes, and swamps. The wetlands provide plenty of food for these animals, and are a good place for them to raise their young.

● Wetlands are good food-stops for birds that fly long distances. They often stop over on long flights to rest or feed before going on with their journey.

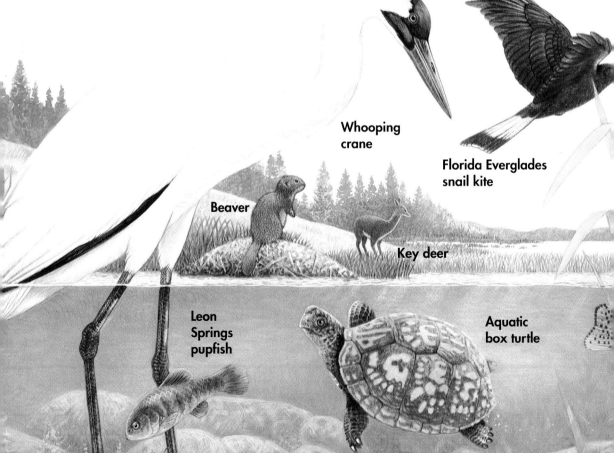

**Whooping crane**

**Florida Everglades snail kite**

**Beaver**

**Key deer**

**Leon Springs pupfish**

**Aquatic box turtle**

• Alligators were once hunted for their skins. By the 1960s they were endangered, and the hunting was stopped. Now their numbers are rising again.

# Which orphans are fed by puppets?

In some Russian wetlands, people are caring for Siberian crane chicks whose parents have been shot. These human "moms" wear sheets over their heads and puppets on their hands. The chicks think they're being looked after by real birds and are more likely to join a real flock when they grow up.

Wood stork

Schaus's swallowtail butterfly

Green-backed heron

Marbled teal

Apache trout

American crocodile

# Why are boats bad for manatees?

Manatees are gentle animals—they spend their lives swimming along, grazing on sea grass. Unfortunately, they share their waterways with fast-moving boats, and many manatees are injured by propeller blades. This means the animals are getting rarer.

● The Chinese river dolphin is endangered. It is almost blind and uses sound to find its food. The sounds of boat engines confuse it, and it swims the wrong way—sometimes into fishing nets.

# Where do sturgeons' eggs go?

Every year sturgeons swim from the sea to the rivers where they were born to lay their eggs. Many don't make it—they are caught for their eggs. The eggs are sold as the luxury food "caviar," and end up on crackers at parties.

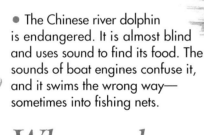

# Why should you keep quiet about olms?

Collectors have taken so many of these blind, cave-dwelling salamanders from underground rivers that they are now very rare. So when people find them in new, safe places, they should keep it a secret.

● In a sea-life hospital in Florida, injured manatees wear life jackets to keep them afloat while they get better.

# How can fish make an eagle sick?

● In Europe, river otters nearly died out because their rivers were so polluted. But some of the rivers have been cleaned, and the otters are coming back.

The bald eagle was endangered when its fish suppers were poisoned by crop spray. The spray had washed off the land into lakes and into the fish. When the poison was banned, the fish and the eagles thrived once more.

# Which endangered animal has a magic horn?

Rhinos live on the grasslands of Africa and Asia. It is against the law to hunt them, but some people still do because they can get a lot of money for a rhino's horn. In some countries the horn is thought to have magical powers, and is carved into dagger handles or ground up for medicines.

● In some African nature reserves the rangers catch the rhinos and cut off their horns. It doesn't hurt the rhinos, and hopefully it will stop poachers from killing them.

● The African pancake tortoise is endangered because so many are caught to be pets. In the wild it gets away from its enemies by hiding between rocks. It may fool other animals, but this trick doesn't work against pet hunters.

• Like many grassland animals, the great bustard is becoming endangered as its home is turned into farmland. Cattle tramp on the nests and escaping birds often fly into overhead cables.

# Where can you shoot elephants?

Elephants are endangered because so many are killed for their ivory tusks. In most places it is against the law to shoot them—except with a camera. The money tourists pay to see elephants in reserves can be spent on protecting the elephants from poachers.

# Which "extinct" animal returned to the wild?

Père David's deer was once extinct in the wild. The only ones left lived in zoos and parks. Luckily they were bred so successfully that now they are being returned to their grassland homes in northern China.

# Why do orangutans need all the trees?

Orangutans are rain forest animals that spend all their lives in the trees. When trees are cut down, gaps are left in the forest, and orangutans can't cross the gaps to find food or places to sleep.

● There are more kinds of trees and animals in the rain forests than in any other place. When the trees are cut down, all the living things in the forests are in danger.

# Which endangered animal is the shyest?

The shy okapi is so hard to find that scientists didn't even know it existed until 1901. Today there are fewer okapis than ever, because their rain forest home is being cut down.

# Why is it bad luck to be an aye-aye?

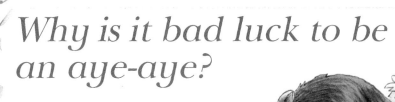

Aye-ayes feed at night in the rain forests of Madagascar. Some of the people of that island think that aye-ayes bring bad luck, so they kill them. The animals are extremely rare, but in some places they are now protected.

● Rain forest hunters have used poison from poison dart frogs on the tips of their arrows for centuries. But now the frogs are in danger from collectors selling them as pets.

# Which fox flies to its food?

The Rodrigues flying fox isn't a fox—it's a bat that lives on Rodrigues island in the Indian Ocean. It eats fruits, so it needs lots of fruit trees. Sadly, most of its forest home has been cut down, and there are now only a few thousand of these bats left.

# Why are polar bears still at risk?

Polar bears used to be hunted for their fur. That has stopped now and the biggest threat to them is the planet overheating due to pollution in the air. If the Arctic ice melts, the bears won't be able to roam freely in search of food.

# Why do seals get their fur dyed?

In some areas of the Canadian Arctic, the pups of ringed seals are hunted for their pure white fur. People trying to protect the seals sometimes spray them with colored dye. It doesn't hurt the baby seals but it makes the fur useless to the hunters.

● In some areas, polar bears go into towns to scavenge for food. Hungry bears can be a danger to people. Some have to be shot, but most are just taken somewhere safer.

● People nearly hunted the musk ox to extinction until they realized they'd make more money from its thick, soft fur than from its meat. They stopped killing the ox and now shear it like a sheep instead.

# Which endangered whale has a unicorn's horn?

The narwhal is a kind of whale that lives in the Arctic seas. The male is hunted for its spiraled tusk, which looks just like a unicorn's horn. If too many narwhals are taken, they may one day become extinct.

● Antarctica hasn't suffered as much from the harmful things that humans have done as other parts of the world. It is the last wilderness, and many think it should stay that way.

# What's so "right" about the right whale?

The right whale got its name from the people who used to hunt it, the whalers. They said it was the right whale to catch, because it gave lots of useful whalebone and oil. So many were killed that it became endangered. Most hunting stopped 60 years ago, but these whales are still very rare.

● The Inuit people of the Arctic still hunt right whales. They are allowed to because it is part of their traditional way of life. Some people think this should be stopped too.

● If modern fishing boats carry on catching as many fish as they are catching now, there'll come a day when all the boats will be trawling for the same few fish.

● People have always been scared of great white sharks, but the sharks have more reason to be scared of us. Many are hunted every year, and their teeth and jaws are sold to make expensive trinkets.

● At certain times large bands of crown of thorns starfish feast on coral—causing great damage to coral reefs. This may be because fishing boats are catching too many of the starfish's natural enemies.

# Do oceans have parks?

You can visit parks under the sea as well as on land. The largest of these underwater reserves is the Great Barrier Reef off the coast of Australia, which was made to protect the coral reefs and wildlife there.

● Every year millions of sea creatures die because they are trapped in garbage made of plastic. Turtles often choke on plastic bags, thinking they are yummy jellyfish.

# When do parrots make bad pets?

Parrots make bad pets when they are taken from their natural homes. Every year thousands of parrots are taken from the wild. They are often carried to other countries in cramped boxes. Many die before they even get there, and others soon after.

PET STORE

● An animal that is taken from its natural home is less likely to survive than one that's been born and bred by people. If you want a pet, make sure it isn't a wild animal.

● Spix's macaws have been highly prized as pets. Today there are only around 50 left, but none of them live in the wild. The last known Spix's macaw disappeared from northeast Brazil in 2000.

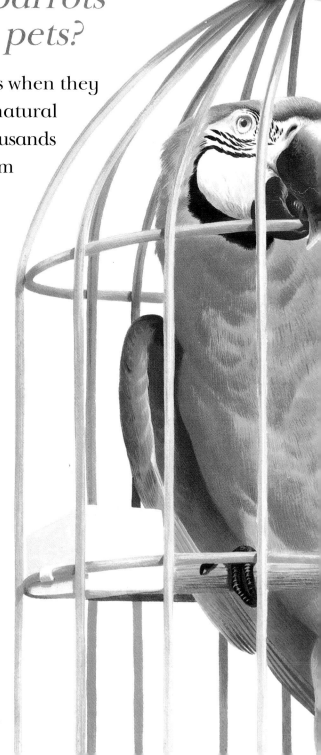

● It is a good idea to find out how large your pet will become before you buy it. People are often surprised when the small pet they took home grows into a monster!

# Who carries a chameleon in a suitcase?

Vacationers have been caught with chameleons in their suitcases. It's against the law to take endangered animals from one country to another. These people wanted to smuggle the lizards home.

● Chimps, macaques, and tamarins are often kept by scientists who test their new medicines on them. Some people say this must be done to make sure that medicines are safe for people. Others say it is cruel and should be stopped.

# How could a bonfire save elephants?

The president of Kenya once set fire to 12 tons of elephant tusks, worth over $2,000,000. The tusks had been taken away from poachers. By burning them, Kenya was saying to the world that it thought buying and selling ivory was wrong. It was hoping to persuade other countries to stop the trade in ivory and do more to protect the elephants.

# Who grabs robber crabs?

Robber crabs live on islands in the Pacific and Indian oceans. Some grow up to three feet across. They are hunted for food and made into souvenirs for tourists.

● At nearly six feet long, the Chinese giant salamander is the world's largest salamander. So many people enjoy eating it that it has become endangered.

# Why would leopards rather not be spotted?

Some people like to wear coats made of beautifully spotted leopard skin. Others hunt big cats because they find it exciting. If the leopards had a voice, they might say they'd rather have plain fur that nobody wanted to wear.

# Why do tigers need corridors?

In India, many tigers live in reserves and national parks where they are safe from hunters. The problem is that one park is often cut off from another. A "corridor" is a strip of forest linking two parks. Tigers can travel along it to find food or mates.

# How does a possum cross the road?

Today the rare mountain pygmy possums of Australia use an underpass! When a road was built through their reserve, many males were hit by cars when they went to visit the females. A tunnel was built for them to cross the road safely.

● The Galápagos Islands in the Pacific Ocean have plants and animals on them that are not found anywhere else in the world. The islands have been turned into a huge national park so all the wildlife is protected.

# Why are gorillas not to be sniffed at?

Mountain gorillas live in reserves high up in the Virunga Mountains in Africa. People can visit them, but the gorillas are not used to common human illnesses. They can die of the flu. To protect the gorillas, visitors have to show that they're fit and healthy.

● There are probably fewer than 2,000 tigers left in India. They are protected by law, but poachers still kill them because their claws and bones can be sold to make medicines, and the fur sells for a lot of money too.

# When do animals like going to the zoo?

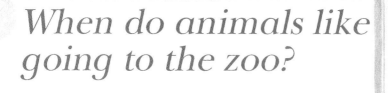

In the past, zoos kept animals just for people to look at. To some people, the animals looked cramped and lonely. Today, many zoos are working hard to breed endangered animals, such as tamarins, so that they can return them to the wild.

# When do animals like leaving the zoo?

The last wild Arabian oryx was shot in 1972—others were rescued and were kept in zoos. They bred and now a herd of around 100 roams the deserts of Oman once more.

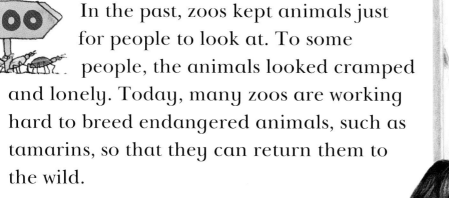

● Sixty-five years ago, the golden hamster was nearly extinct. Then one female and her 12 young were caught and allowed to breed in safety. Soon there were millions of them!

# Which endangered animal is brought up in a bucket?

Kemp's ridley turtles are being raised in special hatcheries in Texas and Mexico. In their buckets, they are safe from seabirds and other hunters. When they are big enough to fend for themselves, they are put into the ocean.

● Everyone thought the bridled nailtail wallaby, or flashjack, was extinct. Then a colony was discovered in 1973 near Dingo in eastern Australia. The area where they live is now protected.

# Why do animals need us?

In most cases, animals become endangered because of things that people do. Animals cannot speak, so they need us to speak for them. Most of all, they need us to stop doing the harmful things we do and help keep them safe.

● Lots of people are helping animals in danger. If there's an oil spill, for example, teams work hard to clean the animals so that they can be returned to the wild.

● Everyone can help save endangered animals. We can join groups that are trying to protect them. We can be careful about the things we buy, and we can take less from the natural world and make less mess.

# Why do we need animals?

Some wild animals provide us with food, clothing, and other materials. If they disappeared, we'd lose those things. Animals make the world a beautiful and interesting place. Doesn't it make sense for us to take care of them?

● Many people believe we should save animals just because they exist, and that they have as much right to be on this planet as we do. Shouldn't we treat them with the same kindness as we'd wish for ourselves?

# Index